Grandfather's Tiger Tales

Anjana Basu

Illustrated by

Aaryama Somayaji

talking CUB

An Imprint of Speaking Tiger Books

TALKING CUB

125A, Ground Floor, Shahpur Jat,
Near Asiad Village, New Delhi - 110 049

First published in paperback in Talking Cub
by Speaking Tiger Books in 2022

ISBN: 978-93-5447-275-6

eISBN: 978-93-5447-283-1

10 9 8 7 6 5 4 3 2 1

Typeset in Cardo by Jojy Philip
Printed at Sanat Printers, Kundli

Anjana Basu works as an advertising consultant in Kolkata. She writes stories and features in the local newspapers and for *Outlook* and *Statesman.* She is the author of a number of novels, children's books and short story collections. Some of her books for children include *In the Shadow of the Leaves, Leopard in the Laboratory, Eighteen Tides and a Tiger, Hide and Seek Tiger, Lockdown Tiger* and *Chinku and the Wolfboy.* In 2004, she was awarded a Hawthornden Fellowship in Scotland where she worked on her second novel, *Black Tongue.*

Aaryama Somayaji studied Communication Design at the National Institute of Design, Vijayawada. She draws to survive, reads for herself, and eats to stay happy. Illustrating for children is her way of giving back the joy she had as a child. She can usually be found reading in her room or looking at cat videos on the Internet.

For Rahul, Rudra and Rohan,

my 3 'R's and for Sreeja, who would much

rather be known as Oro.

Contents

Introduction

These stories came about as a result of a collection of snippets on tigers that I posted on Facebook. They are all linked to the Sundarbans in one way or the other and they go to prove that nature does not always behave in the way you expect.

Of the three stories in the book, two actually did happen.

The account of the tiger that came to a cricket match is recorded in the archives of one of the earliest clubs set up by the British—the Calcutta Cricket and Football Club (CC&FC).

In 1756, when Siraj-ud-Daulah took back the city of Calcutta (now Kolkata) from the British, what is now Salt Lake was the main part of the city and the Lower South Circular Road, which is now known as Chowringhee, formed the city's southern border. Beyond that were the forests of Sundarbans, and it was believed that tigers stalked those forests... Names like Creek Row and Canal Road go to show that the creeks and canals of the Sundarbans had possibly sent their sinuous tentacles into the city—crocodiles and all.

This explains why when the teams Bally and Saugor, named after islands in the Bay of Bengal, were engaged in a heated competition on an open ground near the river, the cricket match had an unexpected onlooker. A tiger ambled lazily out of the nearby jungle. After this incident, the Club quickly found a safer ground in the heart of Ballygunge, where they set up the bungalow that they currently occupy.

The second story in this collection is taken from *Bon Bibi Johuri Nama,* a series of verses in honour of Bon Bibi, the goddess of the Sundarbans. It tells of the plight of poor Dukhi who finds himself facing the fangs of Dakshin Ray, the tiger god. Dukhi calls on Bon Bibi for help.

Bon Bibi, Sundarbans folklore has it, was sent by Allah to protect the forests. She and her twin brother Shah Jongoli came all the way from the holy city of Medina. An archangel brought them the message that they had been chosen for a divine mission: they were to travel from Arabia to the 'country of eighteen tides'—*atthero bhantir desh*—in order to make it fit for people to live in. This included fighting Dakshin Ray and his army of ghost tigers.

The *Johuri Nama* was composed sometime in the late eighteenth century and what makes it remarkable is the ending of the Dukhi story, something that relates directly to today's world of man-animal conflict.

The third story relates something that happened as a result of Cyclone Aila which lashed the Bengal coastline in 2009. After the cyclone, as the Sundarbans pulled itself back together, the tale of a man in Amlamethi on the West Bengal side of the mangroves, who found himself sharing four walls and a string bed with a tiger, began to spread like wildfire.

The Sundarbans is famous for its tiger attacks. As early as 1666, the French explorer Francois Berniere reported that natives of the Sundarbans were constantly in danger from tigers. Some say that the tiger's dharma is to hunt and because it hunts, it acts as the guardian of the Sundarbans. People remain vulnerable, thanks to the many creeks down which the tigers swim, ignoring crocodiles, to reach the villages.

However, the result in this case was rather unexpected and only goes to prove that fiction like *Life of Pi* does have foundation in fact.

However, to find out what happened, as with all stories, you'll have to read it.

Happy wanderings through tiger territory.

The Tiger That Came to the Cricket Match

What would happen if a tiger walked into a cricket match? Rohan thought idly as he sprawled on the grass waiting to bowl. It was a warm lazy afternoon and neither the batsmen nor the bowlers seemed to be in any hurry to make runs or take wickets. The cricket field was lined with trees and the sunlight bounced off the leaves making the shadows beneath the trees dance. Perhaps that was why he had thought of tigers—that and Dadubhai telling him shikar stories.

Dadubhai had once been a shikari himself. 'I don't think it's a good thing, mind you,' Rohan's grandfather told him. 'But we were all taught to shoot when we were young. And before you ask, I didn't shoot tigers.' Dadubhai was well over six feet tall and not at all like a frail old grandfather. Rohan envied him his height. He himself was five feet, two inches and his coach told him that was short for a pace bowler. Rohan however believed in sticking to it despite his mother darkly pointing out that grades were far more important and everyone wasn't Sachin Tendulkar.

The coach called his name and Rohan walked over to the pitch, dusting the grass from his trousers. Neatly catching the ball, he winked at Suresh who was batting and began his run-up. The tiger in the shadows vanished from his thoughts.

'I was Man of the Match, Dadubhai,' he announced proudly to his grandfather, bouncing into the study where Dadubhai spent his evenings. The room was lined with bookshelves, many of the books leatherbound and old. Rohan loved the smell of old books and always took a deep breath when he came into the study. His grandfather smiled, 'That means a treat is due! Come and tell me all about it. Unless you have homework to finish.'

'Ma's gone to the Club,' Rohan said cheerfully and plonked himself in a deep leather chair. He stretched blissfully and began to give his grandfather a ball-by-ball commentary. But somewhere in the middle of his account of how he ran out Suresh for a duck, he remembered the tiger in the shadows.

Dadubhai sat back and listened, a smile on his face. 'Well, I hope Suresh forgave you for running him out but your tiger theory isn't that odd, you know. A tiger did come to a cricket match once.'

'Huh?' Rohan exclaimed.

Dadubhai nodded. 'That's right. It was a CC&FC cricket match.' Rohan had played cricket at the Calcutta Cricket and Football Club or CC&FC, as everyone called it. He had also been to birthday parties there. He stared at his grandfather. 'Where would a tiger come from?' he asked. 'You're pulling my leg.'

His grandfather smiled, 'No, not at all. And no it didn't escape from Alipore Zoo either, if that's what you're thinking. It happened a long time ago.' He sat back in his armchair and his gaze wandered to the ceiling.

'When CC&FC was first founded, it didn't have a club house like the one you see today. The year was 1792. The British were very new to India and trying to make themselves feel at home. So they thought setting up a club would be good. The members could play cricket and they would have matches beside the river because the fields were wide and there was lots of space.

'It happened on a day in spring, much like this one. Teams would invite each other to take part. Everyone would pack hampers and fill flasks with lemonade. The ladies would bake or get their khansamas to cook all kinds of things so that they could spend the day having fun while the gentlemen batted and bowled and showed what sporting heroes they were.'

'What did they wear to play cricket?' Rohan wanted to know.

Dadubhai frowned thoughtfully, deepening the wrinkles on his forehead, 'Well, there were no pads and helmets. They wore white yes, but loose trousers and full-sleeved shirts with top hats or caps on their heads. Some of them even tied a sash in their team's colours around their waist, which they had learnt to call cummerbunds in the language of their Indian manservants or bearers.

'Anyway, this particular match was being played between the Cricket Club and the Gentlemen of Bally or Saugor, or something like that. The coachmen who were driving the horse-drawn coaches had stationed them all around the grounds. The ladies were seated on the grass, their skirts spread out like huge flowers. Some ladies preferred to watch the match from the coaches where they had a better view of the match and where the grass wouldn't stain their linen.

'There weren't any pace bowlers in those days nor did the players have those swanky curved cricket bats that you wave around now. Their bats were shaped from willow wood, which is why they are also called willows. And they would get their bearers to oil the bats carefully. The Cricket Club team would have their bearers lined up on Sunday mornings with the bats and oil while they and their memsahibs went to church. This way the memsahibs would not have a chance to complain that the bearers were wasting valuable time which they could have spent polishing candlesticks at home because the bats would be oiled and back in their stand by the time all the sermons were over.

'Anyway, the day was sunny and the match was slow. The first wicket took forever to fall and one of the players who was waiting to come on could be heard snoring. The Cricket Club captain glared in the direction of the snores but no one paid any attention. Finally, just before the spectators began fidgeting for lunch, one of the bowlers bowled a yorker at Captain Goode who was on his way to scoring twenty-five. Goode mistimed his strike and tried to hit it for a six.

'The fielder at extra cover leapt into the air to catch the ball and fell, twisting with it to the ground. The bowler threw up his hand shouting, "Howzat!" When the batsman began to walk away there was a roar from the Cricket Club team and a faint patter of clapping from the ladies. And that was when certain people became uneasily aware that there was a spectator whom no one had bargained for.

'Something orange glinted in the golden sunlight filtering through the trees fringing the pitch. A shape was sitting quietly between the gnarled hanging roots of a banyan tree, perfectly camouflaged by the sunlight and shadow. The orange of its hide was catching the rays of the sun and shining like gold. No one was quite sure how long the tiger had been crouching there watching the match. One of the bearers who was doing duty as fielder gestured frantically at the captain and finally managed to catch the eye of one of the batsmen. The fielder who had caught Captain Goode fell flat on his face and stayed there, not daring to breathe.

'The other club bearers and coachmen had realized what was happening. Luckily the horses had not caught wind of the presence, otherwise there would have been panic. Nonetheless, the coachmen began fussing with their charges just in case, exchanging glances with the bearers and wondering whether to inform the sahib log. One of the sahibs spotted the tiger and soon everyone was looking in that direction. There were a few faint shrieks from the memsahibs. The team captains who saw themselves as the commanders of the occasion quickly sent whispered messages, advising everyone to stay calm. And given the number of ears those messages passed through, it was like a game of Chinese whispers, though everyone was aware by now that a tiger had come to watch the cricket match.

'In all this flurry the tiger just sat there. Once it yawned and everyone swore later that they could see those gleaming fangs, even the people who were nowhere near the trees...'

'What happened to the batsmen and the bowler?' Rohan wanted to know.

'Well, both the captains were obstinate men and they were sitting together in the viewing area which was next to the river and not near the trees. They both agreed that the match should go on, if only to prove that the British were known for their superior courage. They had defeated Indian rulers like Siraj-ud-Daula and Tipu Sultan by then. So they waved to the bowler to continue.

'The bowler didn't like the idea of running around with a tiger nearby and he looked wildly at the batsmen. "Don't let the side down, man!" the Cricket Club captain shouted, completely forgetting to whisper. That caught the tiger's ear—it rose to its feet and began walking in the direction of the pitch. The bowler and batsmen froze. When it was almost near the stumps, it stopped and looked quizzically at the people all around.'

'Didn't anyone have a gun?' Rohan wanted to know.

'Well guns weren't that common in those days, though yes, I'm sure someone did have a gun,' Dadubhai replied. 'However, I think they were taken by surprise because they had come prepared for a picnic and the only weapons that were handy were cricket bats. The Indians there might have helped but I suspect they were having a quiet chuckle at the sahibs' expense. No one did anything. They let the tiger watch and everyone got hungrier and hungrier while hoping that the tiger wasn't feeling equally hungry. Even the birds, that normally chirped in the trees, and the monkeys stopped what they were doing to watch the tamasha.'

'And then?'

'And then the tiger got bored. Don't forget that it had probably been sitting under the trees for a long time before it had been spotted. It stood and looked around for a while then walked down the pitch and disappeared into the jungle on the other side. The moment it was gone, one of the captains shouted, "Bearer, bundooklaojuldi!" and one of the staff, after decoding what he had said, obediently came up with a rifle.

'Armed with the gun and with the bearers leading the way, the captains marched boldly towards the jungle where the tiger had disappeared. Of course, they didn't find anything and their Indian bearers possibly didn't like leading an impromptu shikar. Finally they returned, too late to continue the match to find that most of the sandwiches and cakes had been eaten and the fielder who had lain flat on his face was busy insisting that he had felt hot breath down the back of his neck with the ladies fluttering around him in admiration.

'He told that story to everyone who would listen to him for many years, and was probably the only one who was really happy about the tiger coming to a cricket match.'

Dukhi and Dakshin Ray

Rohan had gone on a day trip with his class. When he returned in the evening, he was bubbling over with excitement. 'Dadubhai! Dadubhai!' he cried, rushing into his grandfather's library. 'We stopped at a place called Dhopdhopi. There's a Dakshin Ray temple there.'

Rohan's Dadubhai was busy with his files, but he pushed them aside when he heard Rohan. 'I thought the house was too quiet,' he said. 'So you went to Dhopdhopi, did you? Yes, there is a temple to Dakshin Ray there. There's also an area in Baruipur named after him.'

'But isn't he a villain?' Rohan asked. 'Isn't he a big, bad, man-eating tiger?'

'Well, there's a family in Bhowanipore that also prays to Dakshin Ray regularly,' his grandfather replied patiently. 'People choose their gods for very personal reasons, you know. If you want, I'll tell you the story of Dakshin Ray. But perhaps a bath after that trip might be a good idea.' He looked pointedly at Rohan's grimy white shirt.

'Okay,' Rohan said, 'I get it.' And he vanished as suddenly as he had appeared. An hour later, looking much cleaner, he came with his glass of milk and sat expectantly in front of his grandfather.

'Dakshin Ray,' his grandfather began in his most impressive storytelling voice, 'is spoken of in hushed tones in the Sundarbans. No one there wants to say the word "tiger", or even Dakshin Ray, out loud. Some of them carry little chips of sundari wood implanted in their skin for protection, the way you implant tracking devices because, according to the Sundarbans shamans, the chips are a magical shield against tigers. There are some people who think that Dakshin Ray was an actual zamindar rather than a tiger demon, but those are usually historians. For most people he is a demon, or rather some kind of "weretiger" who oppressed his subjects. He would prey on those who made their way into the heart of the forest to collect honey and wood.

'More and more afraid of Dakshin Ray, the people of the Sundarbans began calling on Bon Bibi for protection. Small shrines were set up under trees and stones and inside all the homes. The prayers were so powerful that they reached out to Bon Bibi and her brother Shah Jongoli who were then in Arabia.'

'Arabia?' Rohan asked, rather startled. 'What has Arabia got to do with the Sundarbans?'

'Well, if you think about it, Bibi is a Muslim word. Bon Bibi is the name of a Muslim deity who also happens to be an incarnation of the goddess Durga. But then no one is really bothered about these things in the Sundarbans—you could say it was a form of bio diversity,' Rohan's Dadubhai laughed. 'Bon Bibi and Shah Jongoli promptly prepared for war, arriving in the Sundarbans on the back of a winged horse.

'Dakshin Ray was furious when the news reached him and he started arming his tigers with powerful mantras and getting ready for battle. His mother Narayani Devi pointed out that only a woman could fight a woman and so she would take care of Bon Bibi for him while Ray could concentrate on Bibi's brother Shah Jongoli. When the day arrived, a great battle started. Shah Jongoli took on Dakshin Ray and his tigers while Bon

Bibi and Narayani Devi threw thunder bolts at each other.

'However, all Dakshin Ray's mantras and tigers were no match for Bon Bibi and her brother. Bon Bibi sealed the mouths of the tigers with a single spell. Seeing this, Narayani Devi threw herself at Bon Bibi's feet begging to be forgiven and asking for protection for herself and her son. Dakshin Ray did the same. Bon Bibi, who was very big hearted, as a goddess always is, hugged Narayani Devi and called her "dear sister". She promised that as long as Narayani Devi and she remained sisters, people would worship both of them.

'From that day on, the two became close allies. However, Dakshin Ray was not at all happy with what had happened and he continued to harass all those who were followers of Bon Bibi. She, in turn, with her twin Shah Jongoli remained watchful and kept an eye out for danger and outsmarted Ray's every move.

'At this time, in a village close to the shores of the deep wide Matla River lived a young boy as sad as his name, Dukhi, and his mother. Dukhi's father, a honey collector, had been snatched by a tiger, and the two of them could barely scrape two grains of rice together. Dukhi wanted to go out to work like his father and begged the villagers to take him on their boats when they went fishing or honey collecting. No one agreed because they knew that if anything happened to Dukhi, his mother would be heartbroken. Dukhi's mother spent her days calling on Bon Bibi, asking her to keep her son safe from tigers, crocodiles and the storms of the Sundarbans.

'One day, an uncle of Dukhi's, known to everyone for miles around as Dhona Chacha, came over to ask whether Dukhi would sail with him to the islands on a honey-gathering expedition. Despite his mother begging him not to go, Dukhi jumped at the opportunity—he had never been away from home before and he wanted to see the other islands in the region.

'Dukhi and his uncle travelled in a country boat with a crew of five. They sailed from one clump of forest to another but did not manage to find any honey—or even any tigers, which was good luck for them. One night, Dhona anchored his boat at an island which had a harbour and he and his crew lay down to sleep. Just as he was falling asleep, Dakshin Ray appeared in front of him in his terrifying part-tiger and part-demon form. "You have not," he roared, "asked for permission to enter my territory."

'Most people made offerings to Dakshin Ray before entering his lands but Dhona had forgotten all about that. He crawled on his stomach to touch the demon king's feet, promising him anything he asked for. The demon king had been waiting for this all along. "Give me your nephew Dukhi," he growled.

'Dhona was shocked when he heard that. He didn't know what to say. Dakshin Ray threatened to tear his throat out and Dhona was too terrified to speak. Then Dakshin Ray changed his tone of voice and promised Dhona seas of honey to float his boat on—provided he agreed to sacrifice Dukhi. He was a cunning demon—he knew if fear didn't work, greed might.

'Even then Dhona hesitated, but temptation and fear finally got the better of him. He and the demon agreed that Dhona would sail back to Kedokhali, a particularly lonely island. Dhona and his men had stopped there earlier but had not had any luck in finding honey. Dakshin Ray assured Dhona that this time he would find honey beyond his wildest dreams. Once the honey was gathered, Dhona could tell his men to cast off, leaving Dukhi behind on the island and at Dakshin Ray's mercy. Before vanishing, the demon warned Dhona that if he went back on his promise, the boat would sink and he, his men and Dukhi would all be drowned.

'Dukhi overheard the whole conversation. Frightened and alone, he wept for his mother regretting that he had not listened to her warnings. In the middle of his tears, he remembered that his mother had told him to call out to Bon Bibi if he was in trouble. So finding an isolated spot far from the sleeping crew, he invoked the goddess. Miraculously, his prayers were heard and Bon Bibi appeared in all her shining glory. She told him that he had her protection and there was nothing to fear.

'Dawn broke early and the crew had just about stretched themselves into wakefulness when Dhona gave his men the news that they would have to row back to Kedokhali island. The men grumbled because they had already combed Kedokhali and the only things they had come across were crabs which made for good eating but nothing more. However, when Dhona told them about his visit from the demon king, the men realized that there was no point in arguing. So they prepared the boat to sail and set course again for the island. They were kind-hearted and didn't want to sacrifice the boy to the demon's claws, but their own lives were more important to them than Dukhi's.

'Just to make sure they were heading in the right direction, Dakshin Ray followed the boat. He summoned his subjects, the honey bees, with his tiger's deep purr...'

'Why honey bees?' Rohan interrupted.

'Because,' answered his Dadubhai, 'they are striped like the tigers.'

'Oh,' Rohan said, 'I never thought of that! Is that why there's so much honey in the Sundarbans?'

'Quite possibly,' Dadubhai replied. 'Anyway, Dakshin Ray called up his subjects and asked them to weigh down all trees on the island with hives full of honey. As a result, once they landed on the island again, Dhona's men could not believe their eyes when they saw the hives buzzing with bees. They promptly set to work, loading the boat with the honeycombs dripping pure golden honey—not even stopping to sneak a taste. After a day of hard work, just before sunset, the men were getting ready to leave the island when Ray in his tiger form appeared to Dhona once again. He reminded him of his promise and by way of tempting him told Dhona that he would make far more money if, instead of the honey, his men loaded the wax from the hives on to the boat. According to one version of the story, Dakshin Ray taught Dhona how to extract the wax and separate it from the honey and make candles from it.

'Obedient to Dakshin Ray's command, Dhona ordered his grumbling men to throw the honey into the water. That is why, according to the old folks who live on Kedokhali, the water around the shores of the island is known as Madhu Pani or honey water and is always sweet unlike the kind that flows round the rest of the salty Sundarbans.

'The boat loaded with its precious cargo, the men asked Dukhi to fetch them some timber from the forest so that they could cook themselves a meal. Unwillingly and unable to refuse, Dukhi walked away from the boat towards the forest knowing that the whole thing was some kind of trap. As soon as the boy was out of sight, Dhona and his men cast anchor and sailed away from the island.

'Dakshin Ray, who had been waiting for this moment, pounced on Dukhi. The boy begged for his life. But Ray refused saying that he was hungry and had not eaten all day. Bon Bibi heard Dukhi's cries and came to his rescue accompanied by Shah Jongoli who was armed with all his complicated magic weapons. Dukhi ran into her arms while Shah Jongoli tackled Dakshin Ray.

'The fight went on for days. Narayani Devi, Dakshin Ray's mother finally made an appearance and told her son to surrender—there was no way he was going to win. Listening to his mother, Dakshin Ray gave in and knelt at Bon Bibi's feet. He begged her to look at things from his perspective—people had stopped making offerings to him and he had no food to fill his belly which was why he had to resort to treachery.

'Bon Bibi thought for a while then agreed to spare his life. She divided the Sundarbans between men and tigers warning both sides not to intrude on the other's territory.

'If only humans had listened to her and not grabbed so much from nature everywhere. Now, thanks to climate change, the islands are sinking and men and tigers are encroaching on each other's habitat.'

'If people knew that it was important to live in harmony with nature so long ago, why has it taken us all this while to realize it?' Rohan asked

'Possibly because everyone thinks that old stories are just nice-sounding words and nothing more,' Dadubhai said. 'We can only hope that the world will realize their wisdom before it's too late.'

Tiger in the Hut

Rohan was watching the movie *Life of Pi* on television. Dadubhai found him flat on his stomach, staring intently at the screen. 'Don't you have homework?' Dadubhai asked quietly.

'I'm taking a break,' Rohan answered. His grandfather sat down on the bed beside him. 'I think your mother would be happier if you read the book, and so would I.'

'I have too many things to read,' Rohan retorted. 'But seriously, Dadubhai, do you think anyone could survive in a lifeboat with a tiger? Of course, the boy was a circus boy, but it's just a story!'

Dadubhai thought for some time while looking at the screen—there was a boy in a boat with a tiger. Then he said, 'I haven't heard of a tiger in a lifeboat but yes, I have heard a story sort of like this one.'

Rohan sat up promptly, TV and movie forgotten. 'Where, Dadubhai? Where?'

'Amlamethi, in the Sundarbans.'

'I haven't heard of it,' Rohan said, disappointed.

'Few people have,' Dadubhai replied. 'Amlamethi is one of those small villages in the Sundarbans that few people get to hear of. Your geography teacher must have told you that the Sundarbans is a World Heritage Site. It's a huge marshy mangrove swamp that is dotted with islands and is home to one of the world's largest tiger populations. There are many islands in the Sundarbans and most of the islands have small villages on them. Some of these islands are sinking, some are safe and all of them lie in the path of the tigers of Sundarbans. All day and during the night the tigers crisscross the islands, swimming from one to the other in search of prey. That's why each village has a little shed dedicated to the goddess Bon Bibi. She protects them from tigers.'

'Oh yes,' said Rohan, who had been on a school trip to the Sundarbans, 'Bon Bibi and the tiger god Dakshin Ray.'

'Amlamethi is on the island of Bali. The villagers there have very good reason to pray to Bon Bibi because they are always in danger of running into tigers.

'A group of villagers had come home after fishing late one evening and were walking into their village. There was a large banyan tree at the mouth of the village with a pond just beyond it. It was dark and the only sound was the rustling of the grass in the breeze. They walked past the tree, happily talking about fish and what had happened during the day when they suddenly stopped and sniffed the air. There was a smell of rotting meat. It was strong—the wind was blowing it straight to them. The villagers were scared. Strange smells in the Sundarbans were always cause for alarm. The smell seemed to be coming from the banyan tree. One of the group had a torch and he flashed it. It picked out something twitching among the leaves. First they thought it was a snake. Then they looked closely and realized that it was a striped tail. A tiger was hiding in the banyan tree branches!

'In the Sundarbans, tigers learn to do strange things, like climb trees which they don't do anywhere else in India. The villagers of Amlamethi were quite used to these things. They backed away from the tree and began chanting Bon Bibi's name.

'Their shouts brought the rest of the village running, brandishing flaming torches. They also began chanting loudly. Like the cat it was, the tiger climbed even higher into the banyan tree and then took a flying leap—one that brought it to ground beyond the pond. From there it swiftly sped through the undergrowth and vanished into the mangroves. The villagers heaved a sigh of relief and said a special prayer of thanks to Bon Bibi with offerings of fruit and honey.'

Dadubhai paused here and Rohan looked at him indignantly. 'Was that *Life of Pi*?' His grandfather smiled and shook his head. 'Amlamethi,' he said, 'faces a lot of wind and storms. It has very little protection from the wild forces of nature. At night, ghost tigers call in the forests beyond.'

Rohan looked even more skeptical, 'And how do they know they're ghost tigers? Do they roar in howls?'

'Patience,' said his Dadubhai. 'No, I wouldn't know the difference between a ghost and a ghost tiger's roar, but I met a ghost at Amlamethi. Yes, don't look at me like that. The ghost was very sure he was a ghost.

'This ghost lived in a two-room hut with a cowshed at the side. The thatched roof was falling apart. I met him a few months after Cyclone Aila. Do you remember Aila? That was the first cyclone to hit Bengal after a very long time. It tore across the sky like a herd of wild horses, trampling and tossing the clouds, tearing trees from their roots and throwing them across roads and paths. In the city, people found themselves being blown off their feet while they were ducking falling branches. But in Amlamethi they have nothing, no buildings to block the wind.

'The fishermen saw the clouds boiling over the water and the river beginning to rise. They turned their boats as quickly as possible and headed for the shore before the wind dragged the water to them. In Amlamethi, the banyan tree by the pond creaked and groaned alarmingly. The wind snatched clothes off the lines and knocked pots off the earthen chulas. The schoolteacher understood what was coming and quickly sent the children home. "There's a great storm coming. Run and tell your parents."

'Birds were screeching and squirrels and monkeys were looking for shelter in the tree trunks. The children told their mothers all this as they rushed home. There was an eerie silence that fell before midday. But the silence did not last long—the clouds in the sky and the waves began racing again. The women had hastily stored food and water in their huts and hoped these would last till the storm passed.

'The ghost was all alone in the hut. His wife was dead and his sons had called to tell him that they had taken shelter in a fisherman's hut before the mobile networks went down and cut him off completely. He had shut the cows in as securely as possible and then, having stored food and water with the help of a neighbour, gone inside to sit on the bed. Like all the villagers, he thought that the storm would blow over. But this storm was different—it was not going to blow out suddenly like a candle.

'The lonely ghost felt that the walls around him would shake themselves to pieces. He could hear the wind roaring at his door and could feel it whipping his skin from time to time. The only light in his hut grew dimmer. Just when it was at its dimmest, a shadowy silhouette slinked in from the cowshed. The ghost could hear the cows lowing restlessly though the growing darkness. He could not identify what the shape was—an animal certainly. He clutched his bed and huddled under the kantha he had thrown on it when the storm struck. Through all the smells of salt and smoke and cow another unmistakable smell came to his nostrils—the scent of a tiger. This is the end, he thought, he would be chewed to shreds in the middle of a screaming storm.

'Sweat streamed down his body. He was cramped and terrified of moving. The light grew dimmer and dimmer and then there was nothing, just the ghost of a flame to remind him that it had once been there. And then, eyes in the dark staring at him reflecting whatever light the wind blew in.

'The ghost said that was when he died, though his lips were muttering Bon Bibi's name over and over again silently in the darkness, never mind that his mouth had begun to dry out. The cattle gradually stopped their noises or perhaps they were drowned by the whistle of the wind. Outside, a chorus of ghosts howled. Things thumped into the hut. There were rattles, bangs and momentary silence before the noises started up again. The eyes by the wall held steady, unblinking.

'That room in the hut was probably about the size of a lifeboat,' Dadubhai told Rohan. Rohan was staring at him open-mouthed, the film and his study break quite forgotten.

'Evening was falling, and the darkness outside became darker. The ghost wondered if he had had a nightmare—perhaps he had fallen asleep. But the light showed an alert head turning towards the bed, two golden eyes meeting his.'

'But why do you keep calling him a ghost?' Rohan demanded. 'A ghost wouldn't be scared of a tiger!'

'I'll tell you in good time,' his grandfather said.

'There was no question of moving or trying to eat something. The tiger seemed to have the same idea. It sat there, nose twitching as if it smelt the restless cows but it showed no signs of wanting to rise. Perhaps it had filled its stomach before the storm—tigers did that, not eating for days. The ghost had not. His stomach grumbled and the tiger's ears twitched and its eyes met the ghost's. Feeling bolder, the ghost tried moving his hand—there was a water bottle next to the bed. The tiger's eyes moved to the hand and...was that a slight rumble? He couldn't tell in all that noise. His hand froze. He sat there for a while with his hand not moving, suspended in mid-air. When he saw the tiger wasn't moving either, he stretched out towards the bottle. It took him forever but finally he was able to pick up the bottle and wet his lips, the tiger watching him intently all the while. But he didn't dare do anything about his rumbling stomach. That would mean getting up from the bed and going to the space where his food was kept. In that wind there was no question of lighting the coals of the chula. When darkness fell, the only light would come from the tiger's eyes. The two cows would have to fend for themselves, though there was lots of straw in their stall.

'And when the storm ended? Would the storm ever end? The howls and whistles from outside were still as loud as before and rain occasionally spattered on the dim glass of the window. Nature spitting at man, he thought gloomily, but then it was spitting at animals as well. The mangroves would be uprooted and the rising waves would drown the already drowning animals even further.

'His thoughts wandered for a long while but came back with a start when he realized that the tiger had got to its feet. His heart began thudding, filling his ears with the noise. This was it then, the teeth were going to sink into his neck... His fingers clutched the strings of his charpoy bed convulsively. But the tiger only yawned widely, turned in a small circle, stared at the ghost on the bed and sat down again.

'Gradually his heart slowed and the rumbling stomach took over. Now it was pitch dark. "Where tigers are feared, there darkness is near," there was an old saying that the people of Amlamethi quoted. It was dark, he thought, and there was a tiger.'

'The tiger ate him?' Rohan asked

'No,' his grandfather answered. 'The poor ghost went to sleep. He had been up the night before, wondering what the tiger would do. Despite being so hungry, he went to sleep.

'When he awoke, there was utter silence and a trickle of sunlight. The storm had passed. He was about to leap up, when the memory of the tiger struck him and he froze. Carefully, he raised his head and discovered that the room was empty except for himself. Slowly he got to his feet and went to the window. The tiger had been lying between the window and the bed. There was some scat there which proved he hadn't dreamt it and a pug mark in the dirt. Famished, he groped for food in his kitchen space. With a blackened banana in hand, he stepped outside the hut.

'The world outside was in tatters. The people of Amlamethi were out picking up the pieces. He stood in the shadow of his hut, watching—the sunlight hurt his eyes, but that was how it should be, he was a ghost after all. The woman from the next hut saw him and waved. "Are you all right?" He was surprised that she could still see him. He stood there looking at his hand and then stepped out into the sunlight.

'A long knobbly shadow wavered in front of him. It could not be his. He stared at it for a long time before going to sit quietly in the sun. After a while he would look in on the cows but now all he wanted was the warmth and quietness of the sunlight. The storm was gone. Perhaps it would never return. Perhaps it would return tomorrow. He would remember those two nights forever because ghosts lived forever.

'I met him,' Dadubhai told Rohan. 'When I went to that area to check out the cyclone damage. He thought he was dead. No man could have spent two days in a hut with a tiger and come out alive. The villagers started calling him Bhutu-da, though they made sure he was fed and looked after till his sons returned.'

'Why didn't the tiger attack him?' Rohan asked, fiddling with the end of Dadubhai's dressing gown cord.

Dadubhai thought for a bit. Then he said, 'Possibly because with that storm raging outside, the tiger thought that the man was its best friend. After all, it had taken shelter in the man's hut. Jim Corbett always used to say that tigers are gentlemen.'

Acknowledgements

Thanks to the Speaking Tiger team, especially Sudeshna and my twice editor Renuka for bringing this book to life. Jim Corbett—Carpet Sahib—who, in spirit, has seen me through many books. Vijay, who continues to adore ghosts.

READ MORE IN TALKING CUB

THE ADVENTURES OF GOOPY THE SINGER AND BAGHA THE DRUMMER

UPENDRAKISHORE RAY CHOWDHURY

TRANSLATED BY TILOTTAMA SHOME

The classic story of a group of ghosts, a musical performance in a dense forest, a terrible singer, and an even worse drummer

Goopy Gyne and Bagha Byne have both been banished from their villages for being horrible musicians. They happen to meet each other and become good friends. When they decide to play their music in a thick and scary forest one night, they are heard by the ghosts who live there. The ghosts love their music and the King of Ghosts grants them three boons. With these boons, Goopy and Bagha set out to perform for the king of the land, and earn laurels. But when they scare the king by appearing suddenly in his room, they themselves are accused of being ghosts and locked away.

Will Goopy and Bagha be able to escape and do what they love the best—play music for everyone? Will the two friends stop the kingdoms of Halla and Shundi from going to war? And how many sweets and how much pulao will they be able to eat while they do so?

Upendrakishore Ray Chowdhury's well-loved and hilarious story of friendship, music and magic now appears in an exuberant new translation along with beautiful illustrations. Tune in for descriptions of pots of food and delightful escapades that will keep you laughing till the last page.

HABBER-JABBER-LAW
A NONSENSE ADVENTURE

SUKUMAR RAY

TRANSLATED BY ARUNAVA SINHA

'My handkerchief was somewhere on the grass; just as I was about to pick it up to wipe my face, it said, "Miaow!" So annoying. Why was the handkerchief going miaow?'

On a hot afternoon, a boy sitting in his garden suddenly finds himself transported into a land full of ridiculous creatures talking absurdly. There is the cat that was a hanky. The raven who is an accountant. The old men Uto and Booto who are as bald as eggs and claim to be thirteen years old. And then a sudden commotion about a defamation suit where a barn owl is the judge. Will the crocodile, the frog and the hedgehog ever be able to present their case? And what speech will the billy goat Wren and Baartin BA bleat in the end?

Sukumar Ray's classic work of nonsense *Haw-Jaw-Baw-Raw-Law*, has entertained children and adults for almost a century now. Guaranteed to send you into side-splitting laughter, this iconic piece of literature now appears in an exuberant translation for the modern reader, accompanied by the author's original illustrations.